Linlithgow Palace

Description by the late **J S Richardson,** HRSA, LLD, FSA Scot.
formerly Inspector of Ancient Monuments for Scotland

History by the late **James Beveridge**, MA
formerly Emeritus-Rector of Linlithgow Academy

Revised by **Fiona Stewart**, MA
Assistant Inspector of Ancient Monuments

Edinburgh
Her Majesty's Stationery Office

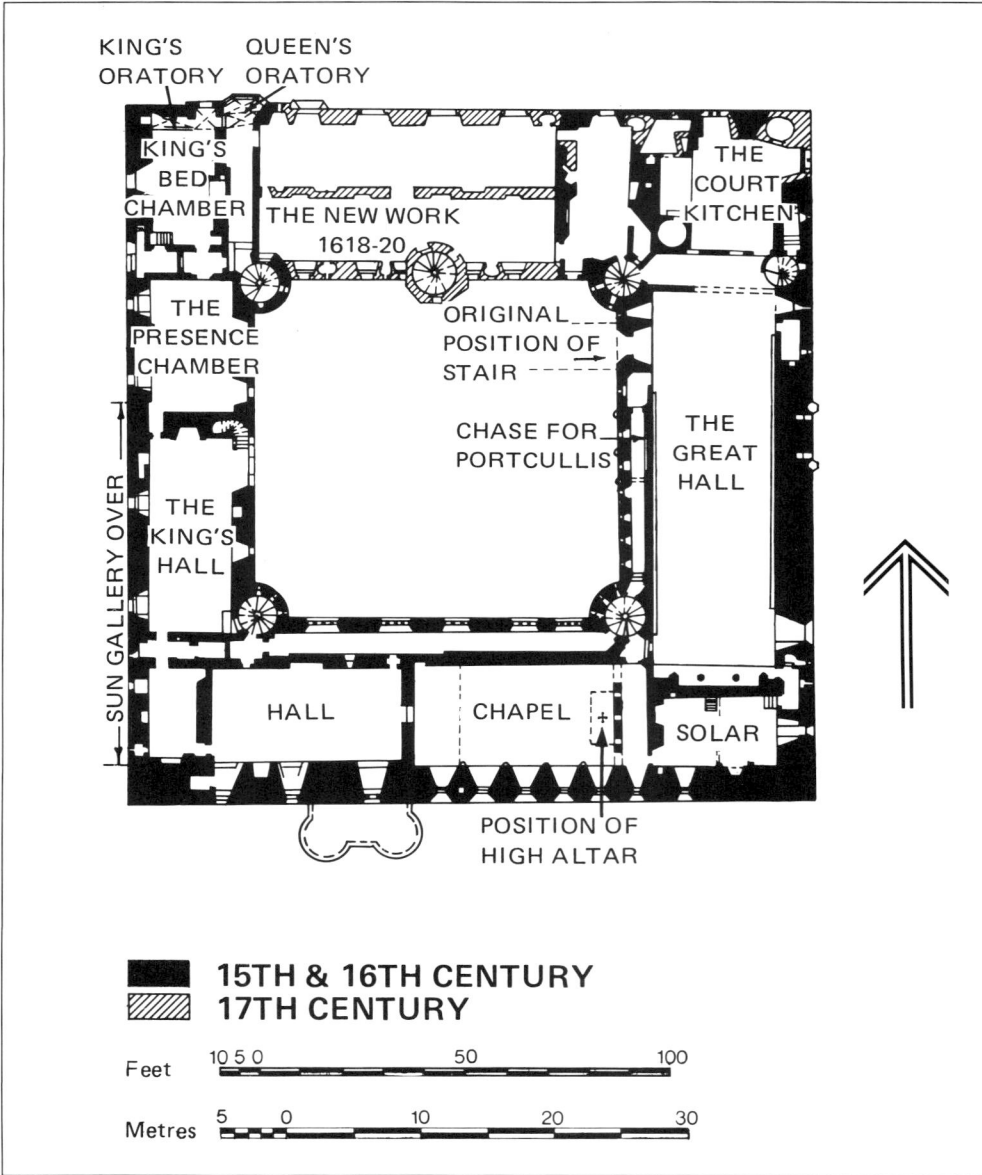

KING'S QUEEN'S
ORATORY ORATORY

KING'S
BED
CHAMBER

THE NEW WORK
1618-20

THE
COURT
KITCHEN

THE
PRESENCE
CHAMBER

ORIGINAL
POSITION OF
STAIR

CHASE FOR
PORTCULLIS

THE
GREAT
HALL

SUN GALLERY OVER

THE
KING'S
HALL

HALL

CHAPEL

SOLAR

POSITION OF
HIGH ALTAR

15TH & 16TH CENTURY
17TH CENTURY

Feet	10 5 0 50 100	
Metres	5 0 10 20 30	

Plan of the first floor.

In the Steps of Kings

Linlithgow Palace, birthplace of James v and Mary, Queen of Scots, is one of the most popular ancient monuments in Scotland. For those visitors who have not much time to spend at the Palace the following short tour is recommended. Used in conjunction with the plans (on pages 2 and 21) this will take the visitor round the principal apartments in the Palace. Supplementary information may be obtained by referring to the relevant sections in the guidebook. The tour should commence at the custodian's office from where it can be seen that the Palace consists of four ranges built around the **Courtyard** in the centre of which is the **King's Fountain**, erected in the 1530's. Cross the Courtyard and ascend the **Kitchen Turnpike** in the opposite right corner, to the first floor. The passage you enter—**Screens Passage**—shielded the **Kitchen** (on the left) from the **Great Hall**, the scene of royal banquets. The Royal Family would have been seated at the far end of the Hall in front of the magnificent fireplace. Leaving the Great Hall by the door on the right of the fireplace, you enter the **Chapel**. It was formerly lit by five stained glass windows between which were statues—now gone, although the bases and canopies survive. Running beside the Chapel, to the right, is a passage which contains a display of objects found on site. Next to the Chapel is a **Hall**, the first of the king's suite of rooms, and possibly serving as the guard room. Moving from the Hall into the west wing of the Palace, you enter first the **King's Hall** and then the **Presence Chamber**. The latter was accessible only to the nobility and in it much of the business of the Court was conducted. Beyond the Presence Chamber is the **King's Bed Chamber**—the Queen's Bed Chamber, which may once have been adjacent to the King's, (as is reflected in the conjoining oratories, or chapels) collapsed in 1607. It is suggested that visitors climb the turnpike stair in the north-west tower to **Queen Margaret's Bower,** from where the layout of the Palace can be fully appreciated. Visitors can return to the starting point of the tour by passing through the north range which was rebuilt in 1618–20 for James vi.

Linlithgow Palace and St Michael's Church from across the loch.

'His Majesty's Palace'

A royal manor-house built of wood and a church of stone were erected on this site in the twelfth century by David, either when he was ruler of southern Scotland (1107–24) or during his reign as King of Scotland (1124–53). The manor-house was probably of the motte and bailey type, a building of wood erected on a mound, with a dry ditch and palisade round the bailey. The motte hill has disappeared but its disposal may account for the great quantity of build-up on the northern escarpment of the promontory. In 1301–2 Edward I, King of England, enclosed the buildings which were there at that time by a peel or palisade with towers of wood, and as an additional protection he made, where necessary, a deep ditch. In the winter of 1303–4, which Edward spent at Dunfermline, Linlithgow Peel was one of the bases of operations for the siege of Stirling Castle which had hitherto defied his efforts to capture it. Siege-engines for throwing stones were conveyed from Dunfermline to the sea and thence to Linlithgow; others were built in Linlithgow. By the middle of May these had been conveyed to the English camp before Stirling. After the surrender of Stirling to the English in August the hay stored in the 'Peel of Linlithgow' was distributed 'among the great lords of the army'.

It was apparently in the late summer of 1313 that William Bunnock, a local farmer who was frequently engaged to deliver hay for use of the garrison, conceived a plan to take the English fortress. Bunnock and some men managed to enter the Peel and successfully captured it and put the English to the sword. Those of the garrison who had been outside engaged in harvesting hay sought refuge, some at Edinburgh, others at Stirling, but many were slain by the country people. The military works were demolished by orders of King Robert the Bruce and Bunnock was rewarded, possibly by a grant of lands in Linlithgow County.

The succeeding sovereigns followed the practice of their predecessors in residing at times in their manor-house of Linlithgow. It was here that Robert II, on 23rd October, 1389, signed the charter that granted self-government to the King's Burgh of Linlithgow. The manor-house had been rebuilt during the reign of David II (1329–71) but it was James I who, in 1425, began the erection of a palace to take the place of the manor-house destroyed by fire in 1424, and it soon became a popular residence for a number of monarchs. Henry VI of England and Margaret his Queen resided in the Palace following the Lancastrian defeat at Towton in March 1461. The Palace was the birthplace of James V (1513–42) and his daughter Mary, Queen of Scots (1542–67). The infant Queen Mary spent the first seven months of her life with her mother at Linlithgow until the Queen Dowager, considering the accommodation in the Palace limited and its situation too exposed in these troubled times, took up residence in Stirling Castle. Following the Scottish defeat at Pinkie in September, 1547, Queen Mary was removed to the Priory of Inchmahome, on an island in the Lake of Menteith, until it was decided to send her to France. Queen Mary's visits to

Mary, Queen of Scots, the daughter of James V, was born in the Palace in 1542. (Reproduced by kind permission of the Scottish National Portrait Gallery)

the Palace, after her return from France, were only occasional when she used it as a resting place on her journeys to and from the west.

The Scottish monarchs who particularly favoured Linlithgow were James IV (1488–1513), James V and James VI (1567–1625). The latter summoned a Parliament to meet there in 1585, an exceptional but not unique occurrence—after the middle of the fifteenth century Parliament usually met in Edinburgh instead of attending the Sovereign wherever he happened to be in residence.

Oliver Cromwell spent part of the winter 1650–1 in the Palace, occupying 'the new work' while the garrison was accommodated in 'the old work'. In fortifying his position he followed the lines of Edward I's circumvallation, constrained by military considerations, but built a stone wall in place of the ditch and palisade. The fort was dismantled in 1663.

Following the Union of the Crowns and the consequent movement of the Court to London, Royal visits became sporadic and the last king to sleep at the Palace was Charles I in 1633. However the hereditary keepers of the Palace continued to live there ready to welcome guests of royal lineage including James, Duke of Albany and York (afterwards King James VII and II) who appears to have stayed in the Palace during the time he spent in Scotland prior to his accession to the throne, and Prince Charles Edward Stewart.

On 31st January, 1746, the Duke of Cumberland's army marched out of Edinburgh in two divisions, one following the coast by way of Bo'ness, the other coming by Linlithgow. Troops bivouacked in the Palace, kindled great fires and carelessly left them burning when they quit their quarters on the morning of 1st February. The straw on which they had slept caught fire and soon the Palace was in flames, and left to burn itself out.

The Palace as a Home

From the time of David I the kings of Scotland occupied their manor-house (later their palace) of Linlithgow at irregular intervals. It was their practice to visit their several houses, partly to supervise the administration of the Crown estates and of the neighbouring districts, partly to consume their rents (paid mainly in kind), and partly for health reasons—with the primitive sanitary arrangements of these days a prolonged stay by a large household soon caused a residence to become unpleasant.

A large number of staff was employed at the Palace to ensure that the comforts of the royal entourage were fully accommodated during their visits: such servants included cooks, cupbearers,

Prince Charles Edward Stewart was the last member of the House of Stewart to reside in the Palace. (Reproduced by Gracious Permission of Her Majesty the Queen)

Illustration of a banquet from a thirteenth century French book—this was no doubt similar to banquets held in the Palace. (Reproduced by kind permission of the British Library)

ushers, a 'Master of the Wardrobe' and even at one time a 'Keeper of the Parrot'. The Great Hall was the function room for grand banquets and minstrels provided music and song from the gallery above. Although these musicians were generally Scottish, there were occasions when Italian, Swiss and French minstrels provided the entertainment. At these banquets guests were served a wide variety of exotic foodstuffs, much of it being imported from continental Europe, including goose, sturgeon, swan, heron and porpoise. Wine was imported from France, Spain and Italy while supplies of beer were brought in from Germany.

Before the Union of the Crowns in 1603 there were few permanent furnishings in the royal palaces with the exception of timber beds, trestle tables, and forms (long seats). Furnishings and hangings were transported with the Court when it moved from one royal residence to another. The hangings were principally tapestries from the looms of France and Flanders and depicted a wide variety of stories and subjects. Beds and chairs were not in plentiful supply in medieval Scotland although the king and queen each had their own. The beds were upholstered and hung with curtains of French silk of different colours with cloth-of-gold and cloth-of-silver as applied decorations and friezes while the chairs were covered with purple, green, or red velvet fringed with silk. In the seventeenth century the Palace was

Wooden panel, bearing the Royal Arms, dating to about 1530. This was probably retrieved from the Palace during the fire of 1746. (Reproduced by kind permission of the National Museum of Antiquities of Scotland)

Head of a lady (height 5cms) dating to the early sixteenth century. (Reproduced by kind permission of the National Museum of Antiquities of Scotland)

scantily furnished but the Governor's rooms in the north quarter were kept more or less ready for occupation. Carved oak chairs of seventeenth century design, coffers (chests) of oak, and aumbries were carried off at the burning of the Palace and some of these may still be in existence.

Certain of the rooms were no doubt panelled in oak but for the most part their walls were covered with a thin skin of plaster, sometimes decorated with patterns in colour, applied before the plaster had set. The floors of the upper storey were of wood and those over the vaults were of stone or tile carpeted with rushes, birch twigs, or bent grass. The upper parts of the windows had leaded glass and the lower parts shutters of oak with most of the windows being protected with iron grilles.

On his visits to Linlithgow James IV sought relaxation from the cares of government and pursued with characteristic energy outdoor and indoor sports and amusements. Archery was practised on the bow-butts—the flat ground to the west of the modern boat-harbour. James lost the stakes in a match with the Keeper of the Palace. He also lost in a match at bowls, played on the bowling-green—the flat ground now occupied by the caretaker's house and garden. Hunting and hawking often occupied the day, dice and cards and dances the evenings.

The fire which destroyed the Palace in 1746 ensured that it was no longer the fairest royal house in Scotland. Time and neglect following the fire did as much harm and the Palace lay uncared for over half a century until in 1832 it was taken over by HM Commissioners of Woods and Forests. Some repairs were undertaken to save the ruin from further decay until, in 1874, the buildings were placed in charge of HM Office of Works.

James V, born in the Palace in 1512, was largely responsible for the final arrangement of the Palace. (Reproduced by Gracious Permission of Her Majesty the Queen)

'A Princely Home'

The Building of the Palace

It was in 1425, following the fire of the previous year, that the building of the existing Palace commenced at the instigation of James I. Between 1425 and 1435 £4,158 was spent on the building, a very considerable sum in those days.

The king and queen frequently visited and inspected the works during progress and in 1434 they supervised the adornment of the royal apartments by Matthew, the king's painter. Floor tiles, probably from Flanders, were supplied via Dundee and paid for out of the king's customs levied at that port.

During the reign of James II there is no record of expenditure beyond sums required for maintenance. James III repaired the building, and, to judge by the money spent, appears to have made certain alterations and additions. James IV, like his great-grandfather, took a personal interest in his palace and improved the arrangements by adding passages, galleries and stairs. From 1502 the master mason at the Palace was Nichol Jackson who was transferred from employment at the building of the Kirk of Steil [Ladykirk, Berwickshire] to undertake special work at Linlithgow. He was succeeded, in 1512, by a Frenchman called Stephen Bawtee [Balty].

James V improved the symmetry of the building by developing it to its complete quadrangular form. He also changed the main entrance from the east to the south side of the Palace where he constructed the existing inner and outer entries. So striking in appearance had the Palace become that his Queen—Mary of Guise—on seeing it, declared it to be the most princely home she had ever looked upon. Sir James Hamilton of Fynnart was made Master of Works and while working under him Thomas Fransh, a French master mason, received a special bounty from the king in consideration of the good work done by him.

Attention was drawn in 1583 to the insecure condition of the west quarter of the Palace but apparently nothing was done. In 1605 James VI was warned that disaster was imminent on the north side of the courtyard. Two years later, on the sixth of September, the Earl of Linlithgow reported to his royal master that 'betuixt thre and four in the morning, the north quarter of your Majesties' Palice of Linlythgw is fallin, rufe and all, within the wallis, to the ground; but the wallis ar standing yit, bot lukis euerie moment when the inner wall sall fall, and brek your Majesties fontan'.

It was not until 1618 that this ruined part of the Palace was taken down and entirely rebuilt under the guidance of the master mason, William Wallace, a sculptor of considerable repute, who had worked at Edinburgh Castle, at Pinkie House, Musselburgh, at Seton Castle, East Lothian, and elsewhere. The rebuilding took two years to complete.

Decay and Destruction

Repairs were carried out in 1628 and 1633 but afterwards the Palace was permitted to fall into a state of neglect. John Lauder, Lord Fountainhall, records in his diary for

An aerial view of Linlithgow Palace and St Michael's Church from the north. The photograph reveals the symmetrical plan of the Palace: four ranges enclosing an open courtyard with a tower at each corner. In the corners of the courtyard are turnpike towers which give access to the upper floors of the Palace.

the year 1668 that 'the Palace, which has been werie magnificent is now for the most part ruinous'. Final destruction followed on the morning of 1st February, 1746. Thus perished the glory of the Palace of Linlithgow along with the dynasty of its founders.

From any viewpoint, but especially when mirrored in the placid waters of the loch, the Palace and church crowning the hill are most imposing and picturesque. The appearance must have been even more majestic when towers, battlements, and roof were complete and when the walls were fresh from the builders' hands.

The Gardens and Orchards

Descriptions written in the seventeenth and early eighteenth-century depict the western banks of the hill as descending to the loch side in the form of an amphitheatre 'with a descent resembling terrace walls' and John Slezer, the Dutchman who was Royal Engineer in

Scotland in Charles II's time, suggests something of this kind in the view of Linlithgow published by him in *Theatrum Scotiæ* (see figure on page 13). It was on these terraces that the king's gardener cultivated the apples, pears, plums and strawberries for the royal table and on which he kept the king's beehives.

Building Materials

The grey and yellow tinted sandstone used by the masons in the various building periods came from Kincavil, a quarry about two and a half kilometres distant; the lime was obtained at Gormyre, near Torphichen. Some of the timber and panelling was imported from the Baltic and Angus slates for the roofs came from Dundee. Iron from Spain was used in the sixteenth century but later this material was imported from the Baltic port of Danzig.

As the church and its yard occupied so much of the limited area of the plateau, the Palace was built partly on sloping ground.

This arrangement, which necessitated considerable underbuilding on its north and east sides, provided a prison and cellars at levels much lower than the courtyard and gave additional prominence and height to the north and east exterior façades.

TOUR OF THE PALACE

The Approaches

The approach to the manor-house had always been from the south but James I having selected the eastern side to be the Palace's main front bought certain lands to enable him to divert the approach road, then called **Palisgait**. This road, instead of continuing as it now does, turned eastward from a point above the present Town House and circled the end of the vicar's garden and the kirkyard. Later, in James V's time, the approach was restored to the original and direct way and is now called the Kirkgait. The **Kirkgait** ascends to St Michael's, a fine example of Scottish ecclesiastical architecture, possibly designed and built by John Fransh (died 1489) father of Thomas, master mason at the Palace. The church is complete with the exception of the open stone crown which adorned the tower. This feature, taken down about 1821, was replaced by a modern spire in 1964.

At the top of the Kirkgait is the gateway called the **outer entry** but also known as the 'foir entress'. Built by James V about 1535, it has on either side of its arched doorway a polygonal turret with gun-ports. The building is surmounted by a parapet, a nineteenth-century reconstruction carried on the original corbel course of rope design, which is twisted and knotted over the doorway. On the south side over this moulding are four panels bearing carved nineteenth-century representations of the insignia of the Orders of Knighthood to which James V belonged. These carvings were inserted in the place of earlier ones which had been destroyed. The pend is ribbed and vaulted in ashlar masonry and

Prospectus Regis Palatis LIMNUCHENSIS. *The Prospect of Their Majesties Palace of* LINLITHGOW.
This plate is Most humbly Inscribed to the Hon.ble Sr James Cunynghame of Milncraig Bar.t

The Palace about 1678 (from an engraving by Captain John Slezer). Note the steep pitched roof of the outer entry.

13

The outer entry, built about 1535. The four panels represent the Orders of Knighthood to which James V belonged—The Garter, The Thistle, The Fleece and St Michael.

The Order of the Thistle from the Outer Entry.

The Order of the Garter from the Outer Entry.

carries three pendant bosses. The first bears a supporter of the Royal Arms 'a unicorn gorged with a crown with a chain thereto affixed, passing over his back and between his forelegs'; the second, a lion rampant, carved in a spirited manner suggestive of the work of a Franco-Fleming, and the third, a running, winged deer-like creature, heraldically used at one time by the Royal House of France. Between the Palace and the outer entry is the **outer close**, once enclosed on its west, south, and east sides by walls and by St Michael's Church.

*The principal features of the **south front** are the five narrow, lofty windows of the Chapel which were protected by projecting iron grilles, and the porch of the **inner entry** with its flanking rounds, built by James V whose coat-of-arms was displayed in a panel over the doorway. Immediately over the porch is a fragment of the battling which protected the wall-walks. The straight joint running up the south-west tower is evidence that James V thickened the western half of the south front.*

*The **west front** is plain and unpretentious. At one time there may have been a wooden balcony, attached to the wall, overlooking the royal gardens. The lower windows on this front were protected by iron bars, the sockets of which can still be seen. The machicolations were probably built in 1504.*

15

In the centre of the **east front** is the doorway of the **old entry** now relieved of its sixteenth-century blocking of masonry. The doorway (see opposite) was once furnished with massive oak doors and within the pend was an iron 'yett' and an iron portcullis of which the chase still remains. A carved panel over the doorway and under a cusped label presents an heraldic display, the principal feature of which is the arms of the Royal House, a shield charged with the lion rampant within a double tressure flory counter-flory. The escutcheon is surmounted by a royal ancient crown supported from above by the figure of an angel with outspread wings emerging from a bank of clouds. On either side of the shield is a kneeling supporting angel and in front, leaning against each of these figures, is a small shield from which the charges have long since been erased. The doorway is flanked by tall canopied and corbelled niches which once contained statues; the corbels are enriched with leaf ornament, the underpart of one being carved with the representation of a man and the other with that of a woman.

The design of each canopy represents in miniature a castle of three storeys, with turrets and battlements. Between the niches and the panel above the doorway are two long vertical slots to house the drawbridge chains. The hinges at the bottom of the drawbridge are still visible. When lowered the outer lip of the drawbridge rested on a ramp, now disappeared, which descended to the level of the Palace gate. To the right of the old entry and connected to the main building by flying buttresses of late date is the ruin of a small barbican or outbuilding. At the southern end, the great east tower, now much reduced in height, dominated the elevation and at the north end the kitchen tower rose considerably above the level of the main parapet, behind which appeared the slated roof of the Great Hall. Immediately below the level of the corbelled course of the parapet walk are six square headed clerestory windows; to the south of these and at a lower level is a large window which lit the dais end of the Great Hall.

The central part of the **north front** is the new work constructed between 1618 and 1620. To the right, on the first floor, is the projecting oriel window of the Queen's Oratory, or private chapel, with the vestiges of the King's Oratory's oriel to its right.

The ground surrounding the Palace is called the **Peel,** a name surviving from the days when Edward I of England constructed the peel or palisade to enclose and fortify the site. On the north side of the peel and close to the shore of the loch are the bow-butts where archery was practised.

The King's Fountain as it may have been in the 1530's (from a drawing by J S Richardson).

The King's Fountain as it appears today, following reconstruction work in the 1930s.

The Courtyard

Before reaching the courtyard one passes through the **porch** of the inner entry where there are wall benches of stone, and gun-ports, and the **pend**, formed from an earlier cellar. A doorway on the east side of the pend gives access to a vault which served as a guardroom, and in the outer wall of which is a fifteenth-century fireplace, not now in the position for which it was intended. Opening off the fireplace is an oven lined with Flemish brick.

In the centre of the courtyard, which was once paved with small stones, stand the remains of an elaborate and curious stone fountain—the **King's Fountain**—once 5·8 m high, the first and finest of its kind in Scotland, and built by James v in the 1530's. In design the fountain is in the late Gothic style but there is a slight trace of the influence of Early Classic Renaissance in some of its details. A spring on the

southern slope of the town supplied the water which was brought in a lead conduit to the fountain and there controlled by a stop-cock. It is probable that adjustable and pivoted metal conduits in the form of long culverin guns, guided water for domestic use from the fountain to portable buckets. At the corners of the octagon were highly ornamented buttresses and crocketted flying buttresses. Those of the upper tier supported sculptured figures of which fragments of a mermaid, a drummer, a whistler and St Michael still remain. The alternate lower buttresses carry heraldic supporters, two being unicorns gorged and chained supporting the Royal Arms of Scotland, one a lion supporting the arms of Mary of Guise, and the third a winged deer supporting the Royal Arms of Scotland impaled with those of France. The pedestals are ornamented with portrait busts in circular frames and also with representations of the lily, thistle, and rose. That on which the lion supporter sits bears figures of nude boys, one playing a lute, one a whistle, and another bearing a scroll. On the pedestal of the winged deer is a sculpture composed of the figures of two gallants in slashed doublets and trunks, holding their sides with laughter, and standing on either side of a twisted column. Above their heads is a scroll from which the motto has been erased.

At each corner of the close are **turnpikes** or wheel-stairs which served the towers and the apartments connected with them as well as the wall-walks. In the centre of the north façade is a projecting turnpike leading to the four upper storeys of this building and its platform roof.

*Over the entrance doorway of the **east front** and forming the central feature of the elevation are three canopied niches. The central niche contained a statue of the Pope, the one to the north a figure of a knight, and the one to the south a representation of a labourer ie 'The Three Estates'. Above each canopy is the figure of an angel emerging from a bank of clouds and holding a scroll. The central angel has out-spread wings and is vested in a cope with rich apparels. Framing all is a bow-shaped cusped label with a corbel in the centre for the support of statues. In detail and character the niches resemble those on the outer face of the entry. The figures on the underside of the brackets represent musicians, and in the central group is one playing the bagpipes.*

*The **south front** was built by James IV, probably about 1500, and is reminiscent of the English style of the period. Direct influence is certainly possible as James IV married Margaret Tudor, daughter of Henry VII of England. Four bracket niches are arranged on the wall over the arched entrance. The upper three supported a group representing the Annunciation, of which the Pot of Lillies and the image of the Virgin Mary still remain. Drawn by R W Billings and published in 1847.* (Reproduced by kind permission of the Royal Commission on the Ancient and Historical Monuments of Scotland)

In the **west front** is a very unusual long window of fourteen lights. This is an insertion between two pairs of round-headed windows and may have been designed to throw light on a carved and painted ceiling in the Presence Chamber. The two large windows near the centre of the façade were introduced in 1620. On the tympanum of the lower of these are the King's initials surmounted by a crown and flanked by scroll draperies. A thistle, a rose, and a fleur-de-lys appear on the pediment. The corbel of the niche over the entrance to the King's turnpike is carved with a figure of Justice holding the sword and scales.

The new work of the James VI period on the **north front** and one window on the west side are in the Scottish Classic Renaissance style then in vogue. The subjects of the carvings over the windows are symbolical of the Union of the Crowns and these insignia were painted and gilded. A few traces still remain of the pre-seventeenth century Palace on this front. Against the north-west stair are traces of windows like those in the adjacent part of the north side.

The Interior

The ground floor of the Palace was generally used for storage.

The **wine cellar**, a large apartment in the basement of the north-west tower, is ceiled with a stone ribbed vault. Here were stored wines from the major European vineyards and the doorway was large in order to allow the free passage of wine tuns. The corbels supporting the central cross-rib are carved with amusing diminutive human figures drinking from large flagons. The cellar and the room to the south can be overlooked from a small entresol within the wall that divides them. The cellar was under the charge of a Master who was assisted by yeomen and grooms. The yeoman of the ale cellar kept the ale and beer, some of which was brewed by the 'Master Brewster,' but a large proportion of the beer in his charge came from Germany.

In the basement of the kitchen tower is the **lower kitchen** and to the south of it another high vaulted apartment with a large fireplace. During the fifteenth century the lower kitchen was known as the well-chamber and contains the draw-well and wall aumbries. The fireplaces in this and in

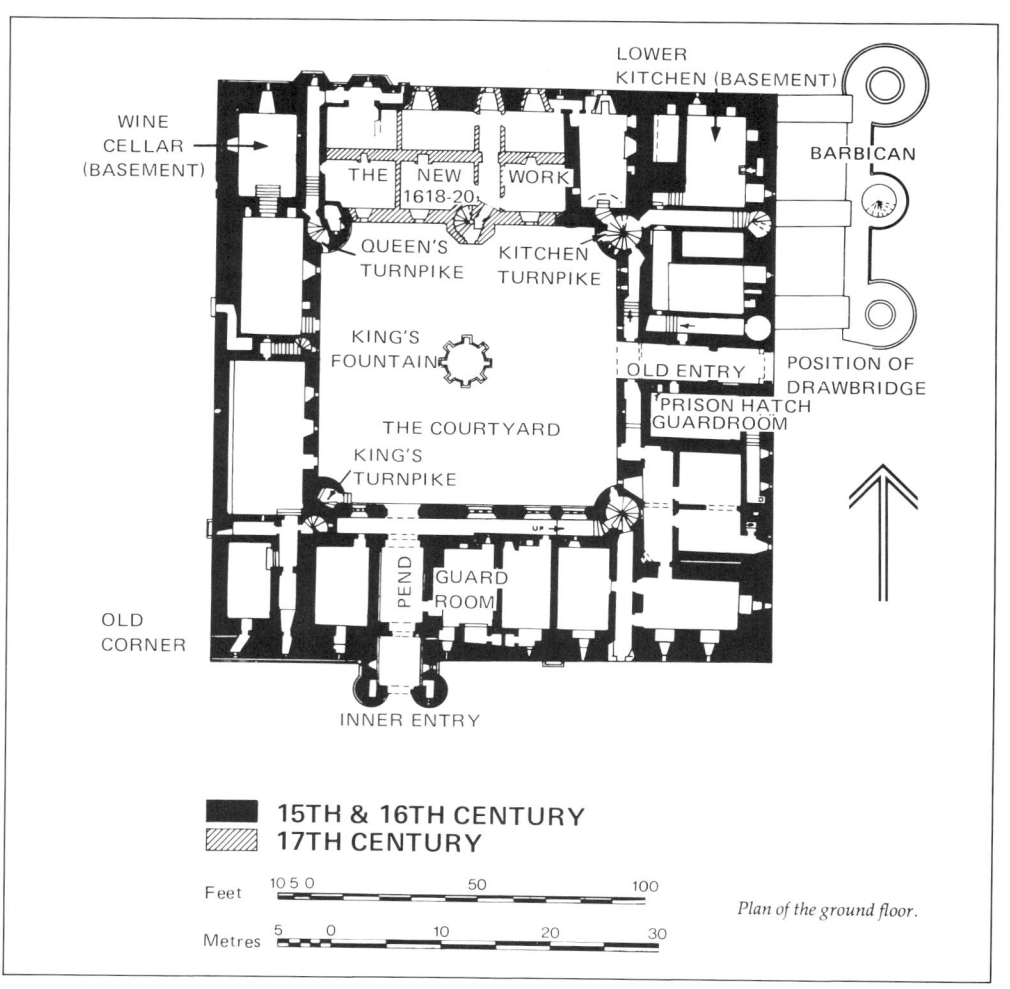

Plan of the ground floor.

21

the other chamber were inserted in the sixteenth century and within their ample jambs stood the great turnspits. A mural passage and stairway leading from the old entry was the original approach to these chambers but when they were made into kitchens the turnpike was built and thus direct access was provided to the servery on the first floor.

The **prison**, situated under the transe of the old entry, is a vaulted pit devoid of any light but furnished with a garderobe. The prisoners were lowered through a hatchway situated in a recess in the north wall of the guardroom which was entered from the pend.

In the north-east corner of the east front, at first floor level, is the original door to the Great Hall. This door was to be blocked and all trace of the stairs up to it removed when the turnpike stairs were added. The six round-headed clerestory windows are a later addition and can be dated to about 1530. Below them is a range of small windows which would light the portcullis chamber of the old entry.

By ascending the turnpike of the kitchen tower to the level of the first floor, the screens passage between the Great Hall and the **court kitchen** is reached. The kitchen lies to the left with serving hatches between it and the passage. Originally it was ceiled with a massive ribbed stone vault, the remains of which are to be seen at the corners. When the tower was heightened the kitchen was remodelled and a new fireplace and ovens were introduced. On the north side of the fireplace may be seen scratchings on the masonry, made by a worker in the kitchen when the great spit turned the roast before an ample fire. A series of intersecting circles, a shield bearing the date 1637 over the initials AW, and a crowned shield with a similar record are to be seen on the springer, and on the arch stone above is 'GOOD [?] COOKE, 1637,' while the same date with the word 'COOKE' is cut on the jamb stone under the springer.

The **Great Hall** or 'Lyon Chamber' (built about 1430), where the Scottish Parliament met in 1585, was entered originally from the close through the doorway at the north or 'screens' end. It occupied the full space between the corner towers and was covered by an open roof of hammer-beam construction but the southern end above the fireplace was vaulted in stone. The lighting was by clerestory windows, five of which on the west side were introduced when a corridor linking the two turnpikes at either end was added. In times of occupation the wall space immediately above the stone wall-seating was draped with tapestries or hangings and the hooks for their support may still be seen. The corbels between the windows, ornamented with leaf patterns, supported statues. At the north, or kitchen, end of the hall was an oak screen which stood forward from the north wall and supported the minstrel gallery which was entered from the clerestory passage. The buffet was placed against the screen and on it were displayed at banquets the 'golden truncheouris'

The Great Hall (built about 1430). The far end, in front of the fireplace, was where the royal family would be seated during the grand banquets which took place in the Palace.

The south wall of the Chapel.

(trenchers) and silver plate. There were two mural pantries near the entrance.

At the south end of the hall was the dais where the royal table was set. The dais was lighted by the great window and backed by an elaborate hooded fireplace of stone above which may have hung the large tapestry from Bruges which displayed the lion rampant of the Royal House. This tapestry, or possibly a carving of the Royal Arms, may have given to the hall the name of the 'Lyon Chalmer'. There are two passages in the western wall, one is at the clerestory-window level and the other on a level with the hall. The latter housed the portcullis of the old entry when in a raised position.

The fireplace, partly restored in about 1907, has three compartments and was the finest of its kind in Scotland. The lintel is supported by moulded responds with leaf-carved caps. The cornice is embellished with leaf-and-stem ornament and over each support is a corbel carved in leaf form. An angel musician, the head of an old man, and the head of a woman, with a small face near her left ear, appear on the underpart of the corbels.

In the east tower beyond the Great Hall are two chambers which originally formed the **solar**. This was to be subdivided when the Chapel was built in the 1490's. One chamber was entered from a passage connected with the Chapel while the other opening off it was also reached by a mural passage in the east wall leading from the Great Hall. The westernmost apartment appears to have served as a vestry for the Chapel and is connected to a garderobe at a lower level and situated below the fireplace of the 'Lyon Chalmer'.

The **Chapel** (built about 1492) has been subject to alterations from time to time with evidence of the ceiling having been altered

The fireplace in the Great Hall. It was partly restored about 1907.

at least three times. Against the centre of the eastern screen wall was the high altar and on the wall above are the remains of iron pins which held the carved retable (enclosing decorated panels) in position.

There was a screen at the west end and a loft in which was erected the organ, made in 1513 by a Frenchman called 'Gilyem', replacing a portable organ.

Each of the five lofty windows contained an image in stained glass supplied by Thomas Peblis, the King's glass maker in the year 1534. On the piers between the windows are corbel brackets for images and over each is an elaborate canopy. The carving on each corbel takes the form of two curly-headed angel musicians. Several consecration crosses are incised on the walls. On the west side of the main entrance to the Chapel is a shield with a mitre carved on it.

To the west of the Chapel is a large antechamber or **hall**, with deeply recessed windows in its south wall, which possibly served as a guardroom. Above it was an apartment of similar dimensions. To the north on each of these floors, and also on the ground floor which contains vaults, is a corridor connecting the corner turnpikes. The first floor corridor now contains a collection of carved stone details, relics of pottery, glass, bone, and metal found during works of repair. In the south-west tower are small rooms furnished with wall aumbries.

Entered from the King's turnpike is a large chamber designated in 1629 'His Majesties' Hall', or the **King's Hall**. At the north end is a handsome fifteenth-century hooded fireplace and there is a small mural stair leading from the east window recess to the cellar below. In the wall to the south of this are an aumbry and a large window; above these, near the ceiling level, are three additional windows probably devised to throw light on a carved oak-ceiling. Two windows with stone seats look to the west. Set into the floor is a flagstone with a series of hollows on it for playing a game. Above this hall is a chamber of equal dimensions with a hooded fireplace similar to that in the room below. At the north-west corner is a mural garderobe.

The next room, which is smaller, is the **Presence Chamber** where much of the business of the Court was conducted. It contains a long and remarkable window. Below this feature are two round-headed windows and a wall aumbry. In the opposite wall are two windows furnished with wall-seats and between them is a hooded fireplace with boldly cut capitals portraying human and lion heads. The fireplace is an insertion and presents the same architectural character as the fireplaces in the James v Palace at Stirling Castle. As late as 1860 traces of colour decoration in orange, red, and black could still be seen on its masonry. The floor of the chamber has been paved with stone quarries and square green-glazed tiles set in a pattern. Floor tiles stamped with the initials I and M tied together by a love-knot have been found in the building and belong to the James iv period.

The room on the floor above is described in the building account of 1633 as 'the great chalmer above the presence'. The windows face the courtyard, the fireplace is in the west wall and at the south-west corner was a passage [now built up] leading to the wooden gallery on the outside of the building. A mural garderobe entered off this passage.

Beyond is the **King's Bedchamber** (including closet and strong room) which leads to the **King's Oratory**, or private chapel. The Queen's suite was originally in the north range—where Mary, Queen of Scots was born—which collapsed in 1607.

To the east of the King's Oratory is a passage terminating in the **Queen's Oratory** with its complete oriel window.

By ascending one hundred and twenty-three steps of the Queen's turnpike the tower-head is reached; the head of the stair is vaulted and the corbels supporting the vault-ribs are carved with the initial M interlaced with an I crowned. An additional seventeen steps lead to **Queen Margaret's Bower**, a small vaulted apartment furnished with wall-seats. Above this was the cap-house, the post for the watchman.

In reconstructing the north quarter a more domestic arrangement of rooms was obtained. The rooms were floored with wood and provided with wall closets for dry stools. The principal apartments were panelled and the ceilings were of ornamental plaster work depicting the royal escutcheon and other devices. The fireplaces are of stone and embellished in the Early Classic Renaissance manner. In 1629 a considerable sum of money was spent on decorating these and other rooms of the Palace with gilt and oil paint.

This sixteenth century red woollen wall hanging, with applied black silk, embroidered with golden yellow silk, is believed to have come from Linlithgow Palace and may date to the time of Mary, Queen of Scots. (Reproduced by kind permission of the Royal Scottish Museum)

Glossary

Aumbry a cupboard or wall-recess

Barbican an outward extension of a gateway

Clerestory or **clearstory** the range of windows in the upper part of a building

Corbel a projecting stone block supporting a member above

Entresol low storey between first and ground floor

Escutcheon a shield on which a coat of arms is shown

Garderobe a latrine

Gothic approximately the period from the late-twelfth to the mid-sixteenth centuries

Machicolation an opening between corbels of a parapet or in a floor, such as a vault of a gateway, through which a garrison could assail besiegers with missiles

Mouldings elaborated profiles which enrich the members of a building

Parapet a low wall, such as that at the edge of a roof

Pend (Scots) a roofed passage through a building

Yett (Scots) a hinged iron grill

Further Reading

H M Colvin, (ed), *The History of the King's Works*, Vol 1, (London, 1963)

S Cruden, *The Scottish Castle*, (Edinburgh, 1981)

J Dunbar, *The Historic Architecture of Scotland*, (London, 1966)

L R Laing, 'Excavations at Linlithgow Palace, West Lothian, 1966–67', *Proceedings of the Society of Antiquaries of Scotland*, Vol XCIX, (1966–67), 111–147

D MacGibbon and T Ross, *The Castellated and Domestic Architecture of Scotland*, Vols 1,2 and 5, (Edinburgh, 1887–92)

C McWilliam, *Lothian* (Middlesex, 1978)

H M Paton (ed), *Accounts of the Masters of Works*, Vol 1, (Edinburgh, 1957)

The Royal Commission on Ancient and Historical Monuments of Scotland *Inventory of the Counties of Midlothian and West Lothian*, (Edinburgh, 1929)

ISBN 0 11 492319 1

Printed in Scotland c.c. No. 18023 Dd. 287272 C52 1/89